NORTH AMERICA AND THE CARIBBEAN

Saint Mary Lake, Glacier National Park, Montana

The World in Maps

NORTH AMERICA AND THE CARIBBEAN

Martyn Bramwell

Lerner Publications Company • Minneapolis

**First American edition published in 2000
by Lerner Publications Company**

© 2000 by Graham Beehag Books

Lerner Publications Company
A division of Lerner Publishing Group
241 First Avenue North
Minneapolis, MN 55401 U.S.A.

Website address: www.lernerbooks.com

Library of Congress Cataloging-in-Publication Data

Bramwell, Martyn.
    North America and the Caribbean / by Martyn Bramwell
      p. cm. — (The world in maps)
    Includes index.
    Summary: Text and maps present the location,
topography, climate, population, industries, language,
and currency of North America and the Caribbean.
    ISBN 0-8225-2911-4 (lib. bdg.)
  1. North America—Juvenile literature. 2. Caribbean Area—Juvenile literature.
[1. North America. 2. Caribbean Area.] I. Title. II. Series.
E38.5 B73 2000
970—dc21   98-048812

Printed in Singapore by Tat Wei Printing Packaging Pte Ltd
Bound in the United States of America
1 2 3 4 5 6 – OS – 05 04 03 02 01 00

CONTENTS

North America 6

The Arctic Regions 8

Greenland, the Faeroe Islands, Iceland 10

Canada 12

United States of America 16

Mexico 22

Bermuda, Bahamas, Turks and Caicos Islands 26

Cuba 28

Jamaica and the Cayman Islands 30

Haiti and the Dominican Republic 32

Puerto Rico 34

Leeward Islands 36

Windward Islands and Barbados 40

The Netherlands Antilles, Aruba, Trinidad and Tobago 44

Glossary 46

Index 48

NORTH AMERICA

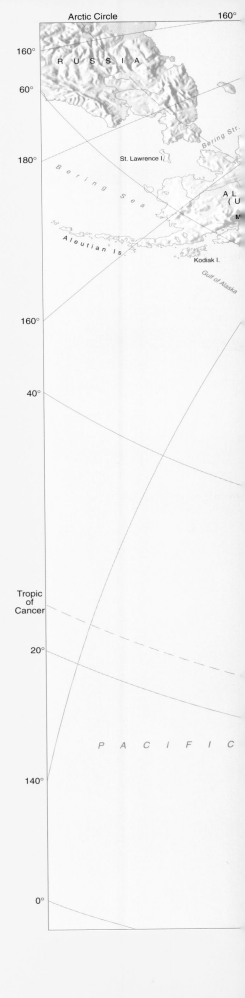

North America is the third-largest continent after Asia and Africa. North America stretches 3,300 miles west to east from the Pacific coast of Washington State to St. John's in Newfoundland (Canada). The continent extends 3,500 miles north to south from the icy shores of the Arctic Ocean to the warm blue waters of the Gulf of Mexico. North America's total land area is more than 9.3 million square miles.

The continent is a land of contrasts, with every imaginable kind of scenery and habitat. Frozen **tundra** (permanently frozen ground) and dark pine forests in the far north give way to the colorful **deciduous** woodlands of New England and the Appalachian Mountains and then to the vast Great Plains of the American heartland. The Coast Ranges, the Rocky Mountains, and the Mexican Highlands dominate the western one-third of the continent. The southwestern states and Mexico contain some of the world's most spectacular desert scenery. The subtropical forests and swamps of the deep south and Florida and the long chain of Caribbean islands complete this kaleidoscope of landforms.

More than 400 million people live in North America. There are 270 million in the United States, 97 million in Mexico, and 30 million in Canada. More than 30 million additional people make their homes on the thousand or more islands and cays (keys) of the Caribbean.

North America is a land of stunning contrasts. People come from all over the world to see the glorious fall colors in New England (*right*) and the spectacular scenery of the Grand Canyon (*below left*). A satellite view of the mighty Mississippi River (*below right*)

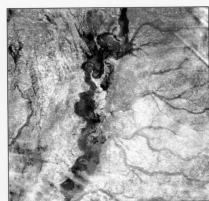

The Arctic Regions

The Arctic regions consist of the Arctic Ocean and the land that nearly encircles it. The northernmost edges of Alaska, Canada, Norway, Sweden, Finland, and Russia form this land ring. Hundreds of islands and island groups called **archipelagoes** dot the Arctic Ocean. The largest island group, known as the Canadian Archipelago, lies off Canada's northern coast. The biggest single island is Greenland. Fewer islands—most notably Spitzbergen (part of Norway) and the three Russian island groups, Franz Josef Land, Novaya Zemlya, and the New Siberian Islands—exist on the European and Asian side of the Arctic Ocean.

Abyssal plains (very deep regions) separated by underwater mountain ranges cover much of the Arctic Ocean's floor. The deepest area is the Pole Abyssal Plain, which plunges near the North Pole to more than 15,000 feet below sea level. The Lomonosov Ridge rises to 10,000 feet and bounds the plain on one side. On the other side of the plain is the Arctic Mid-Ocean Ridge, a volcanic mountain range of molten rock rising through cracks in the seafloor. Shallow **continental shelves**, up to 1,000 miles wide, skirt the ocean's edge. Thick ice covers the Arctic Ocean in winter, but in summer much of the ice melts over the continental shelves, allowing boaters to reach some of the world's richest fishing grounds.

Most of the Arctic landscape is tundra—low plains covered in deep snow in winter and frozen solid for many hundreds of feet down. In summer the snow and the top layer of soil melt, turning the ground into a patchwork of **muskeg** and drier ground clothed in mosses, lichens, grasses, wildflowers, and small shrubs. Native peoples in the Arctic include the Inuit of North America—historically hunters of seals, whales, and walruses—and the Sami (Lapps) of Scandinavia and the Chukchi and Samoyed of northern Russia, who traditionally herd reindeer.

Selected Arctic Facts

• Nearly 1,700 different plant species grow in the Arctic. Almost 1,000 are flowering plants.

• There are about 830,000 native peoples spread across the icy lands of the Arctic regions.

• The highest spot in the Canadian Arctic is Barbeau Peak (8,544 feet) on Ellesmere Island.

• Robert Peary, Matthew Henson, and four Inuit companions are credited with being the first people to reach the North Pole, on April 6, 1909.

• In Siberia, the average temperature in January is -40°F.

• In Russia, the permafrost can extend down to 5,000 feet.

• At 5.4 million square miles, the Arctic is the smallest of the oceans. Its average depth is 4,360 feet.

• Canada's mainland Arctic coastline is more than 12,400 miles long.

About 120,000 Inuit (Eskimo) live in the Arctic regions of Canada, Alaska, Greenland, and northern Russia. Most of them live in towns and small settlements and work in the fishing, mining, oil, and construction industries. Many incorporate the old way of life—fishing, hunting seal and caribou, and traveling by dogsled.

Since 1973 polar bears have been protected by their own international treaty. It has been so successful that the number of bears has increased from about 5,000 to 25,000 in the last 25 years.

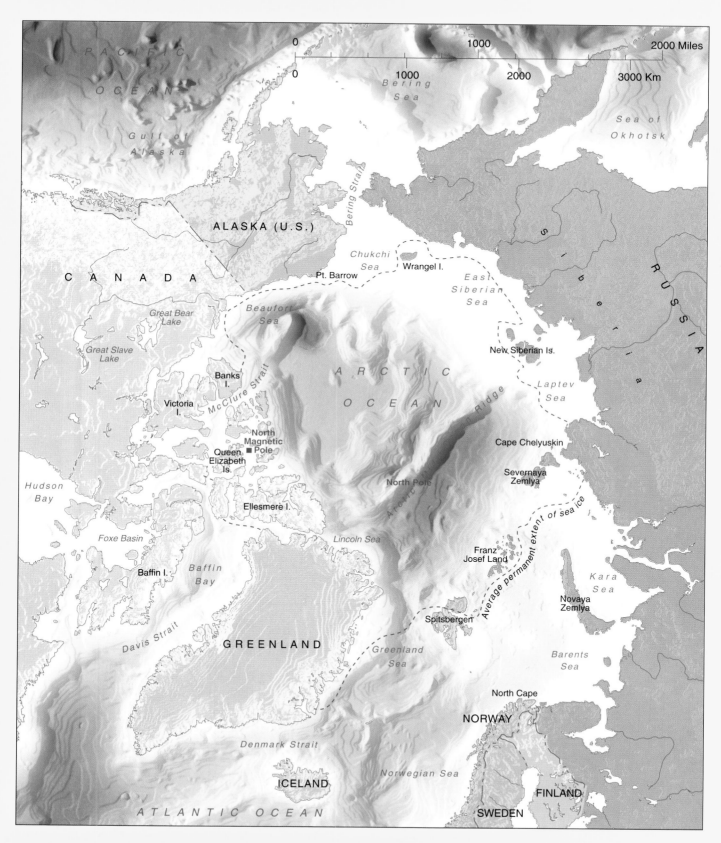

PACIFIC OCEAN

Gulf of Alaska

0   1000   2000 Miles

0   1000   2000   3000 Km

Bering Sea

Sea of Okhotsk

Bering Strait

ALASKA (U.S.)

Chukchi Sea

Wrangel I.

East Siberian Sea

CANADA

Pt. Barrow

S i b e r i a

RUSSIA

Great Bear Lake

Beaufort Sea

New Siberian Is.

Great Slave Lake

A R C T I C

Laptev Sea

Banks I.

O C E A N

Cape Chelyuskin

Victoria I.

McClure Strait

Severnaya Zemlya

North Magnetic Pole

Queen Elizabeth Is.

North Pole

Arctic Ridge

Franz Josef Land

Ellesmere I.

Lincoln Sea

Average permanent extent of sea ice

Kara Sea

Hudson Bay

Novaya Zemlya

Foxe Basin

Baffin Bay

Spitsbergen

Baffin I.

Barents Sea

Davis Strait

GREENLAND

Greenland Sea

North Cape

NORWAY

Denmark Strait

ICELAND

Norwegian Sea

FINLAND

SWEDEN

A T L A N T I C   O C E A N

Greenland, the Faeroe Islands, Iceland

Greenland
(Kalaallit Nunaat)

Status:	Province of Denmark
Area:	840,000 square miles
Population:	58,000
Capital:	Nuuk (Godthåb)
Languages:	Greenlandic, Danish
Currency:	Danish krone (100 øre)

Iceland

Status:	Republic
Area:	38,707 square miles
Population:	300,000
Capital:	Reykjavík
Language:	Icelandic
Currency:	Icelandic króna (100 aurar)

Greenland—in the local Greenlandic language, Kalaallit Nunaat—is the world's largest island. It is 1,650 miles long and 750 miles wide and lies to Canada's northeast. Only 16 miles from the coast of Ellesmere Island, Greenland is a self-governing province of Denmark, which is located 1,300 miles away. Many Greenlanders have both European (mainly Danish) and Inuit ancestors and most speak Greenlandic. Greenlandic place names are replacing most of the island's Danish titles.

A huge ice cap, 5,000 feet thick, covers nearly 85 percent of the island. The only permanently ice-free areas are in **fjords** and bays—mainly along the southwestern coast, where the natural vegetation consists of grasses and clumps of birch, alder, and willow trees. The island has very little farming, but Greenlanders plant a few vegetables and grow hay to feed their cows and sheep.

Greenland's primary industries are fishing and canning of halibut, cod, shrimp, and salmon; hunting for fox, polar bear, and seals; and mining cryolite—a mineral used to make aluminum. The island also has deposits of lead, zinc, uranium, and gold.

The Faeroes are a cluster of 18 small islands between Iceland and Scotland. They, too, are a self-governing province of Denmark. The islanders make a living by fishing, raising sheep, and selling seabird eggs and feathers.

Iceland lies 160 miles southeast of Greenland and 500 miles northwest of Scotland. Volcanic eruptions on the Mid-Atlantic Ridge created the island. At least 200 eruptions have occurred since the island was first inhabited 1,000 years ago. In 1963 an eruption on the seafloor near Iceland created a new island named Surtsey. Ten years later, volcanic activity destroyed part of the town of Vestmannaeyjar on nearby Heimaey Island.

Ice covers much of Iceland, but about one-fifth is rough grassland where the islanders graze cattle and sheep. Islanders produce all the meat and dairy goods needed and export wool and sheepskins. Iceland's primary industry is fishing, mainly for Atlantic cod, and 70 percent of Iceland's exports consist of fish and fish products such as fish oil and fish meal.

The island's volcanic activity creates an endless supply of **geothermal energy**. Steam is piped from deep underground directly to heating and electrical systems in homes and offices in the capital city of Reykjavík. This cheap energy source powers the island's main manufacturing industries—cement making and aluminum smelting (using imported bauxite, the main aluminum ore). Icelanders use geothermal energy to heat greenhouses for year-round food production.

Right: Svartsengi power station in Iceland uses the heat of volcanic rocks to produce the steam to drive its turbines and produce electricity. Water from the Blue Lagoon—a volcanically heated lake—is believed to cure skin problems and other aches and pains.

Opposite: The Icelandic Parliament building in Reykjavík is home to the world's oldest parliament. Called the Althing, it dates back to A.D. 930.

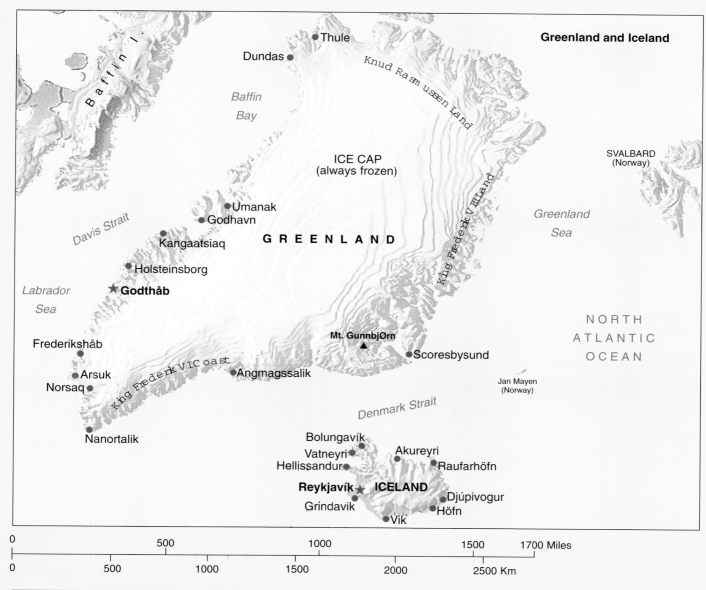

Greenland and Iceland

Thule

Dundas

Baffin I.

Knud Rasmussen Land

Baffin Bay

ICE CAP
(always frozen)

SVALBARD
(Norway)

Davis Strait

Umanak

Godhavn

GREENLAND

Greenland Sea

Kangaatsiaq

King Frederik VIII Land

Holsteinsborg

★ **Godthåb**

Labrador Sea

N O R T H
A T L A N T I C
O C E A N

Frederikshåb

Mt. Gunnbjørn ▲

Scoresbysund

Arsuk

King Frederik VI Coast

Angmagssalik

*Jan Mayen
(Norway)*

Norsaq

Denmark Strait

Nanortalik

Bolungavík

Akureyri

Vatneyri

Raufarhöfn

Hellissandur

Reykjavík ★ **ICELAND**

Djúpivogur

Grindavik

Höfn

Vik

0		500		1000		1500	1700 Miles

0	500	1000	1500	2000	2500 Km

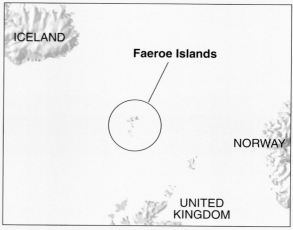

ICELAND

Faeroe Islands

NORWAY

UNITED
KINGDOM

Canada

Canada

Status:	Constitutional Monarchy and Parliamentary Democracy
Area:	3.55 million square miles
Population:	30.6 million
Capital:	Ottawa
Languages:	English and French
Currency:	Canadian dollar (100 cents)

Canada is the world's second-largest country after Russia. This vast expanse covers more than half of North America, from Canada's shared border with the United States to the Arctic Ocean and from the Pacific Ocean (excluding Alaska) to the Atlantic shore.

Canada's far north consists of the Arctic islands and tundra of the Northwest Territories. South of the tundra lies a broad belt of dense **coniferous** forest dotted with lakes and crossed by the country's major rivers, such as the Fraser, the Mackenzie, the Saskatchewan, and the St. Lawrence. Continuing south the forests open to the flat open grasslands of the central prairies.

Canada's west contains some of North America's most dramatic mountain scenery. The Rocky Mountains rise to more than 13,000 feet. Beyond them are the Pacific Coast Mountains and the spectacular fjord coast of British Columbia. Low mountain ranges snake along the eastern half of the country, and gently rolling hills drop to the Great Lakes lowlands, the St. Lawrence River, Québec, and the Maritime Provinces of Newfoundland, and Labrador Nova Scotia, New Brunswick, and Prince Edward Island. The eastern region, claiming some of the most fertile farmland in Canada, is home to most of Canada's people.

An arctic climate embraces Canada's far north. Winters are long and bitterly cold. In the brief cool summer, the average temperature doesn't rise much above 50°F. On Canada's western coast, the Pacific Ocean creates a gentler, wetter climate. Winter temperatures are around 35°F, rising to 65°F in summer. The western region also receives the most rain. Moisture-filled winds blow in from the Pacific and drop their rain over the mountains. As a result, the prairie regions farther inland are relatively dry, with very cold winters. Winters in the eastern lowlands are long and cold with temperatures around 14°F, but the summers are much warmer, with average temperatures of 68°F.

The city of Québec, on the St. Lawrence River, is the oldest city in Canada. Founded in 1608 by the French explorer Samuel de Champlain, Québec City is the capital of the province of Québec. The city has a huge tourist industry, and its busy port handles 15 million tons of goods every year.

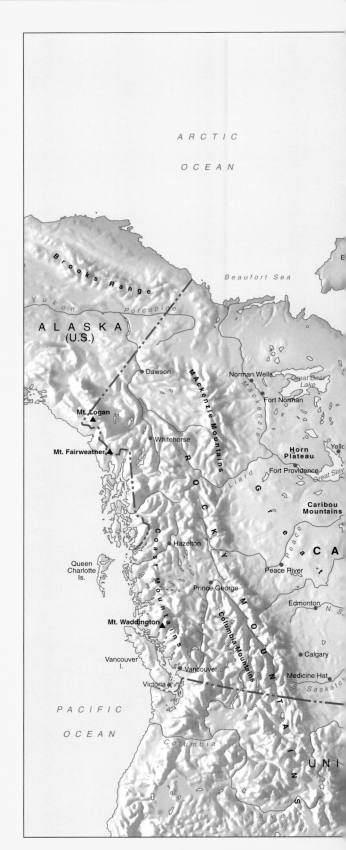

Lincoln Sea

Barbeau Peak ▲

Ellesmere I.

G R E E N L A N D

ICELAND

Melville I.

Devon I.

Baffin Bay

Denmark Strait

Victoria I.

B a f f i n   I s l a n d

Davis Strait

Foxe Basin

Cumberland Sound

Amadjuak Lake

Frobisher Bay

Baker Lake

Southampton I.

Hudson Strait

Labrador Sea

Dubawnt Lake

Coats I.

Mansel I.

Nain

D A

Reindeer Lake

Churchill

Smallwood Reservoir

Happy Valley-Goose Bay

asca

Nelson

Belcher Is.

Feuilles

La Grande

Gander

St. John's

Severn

James's Bay

Fort George

Monts Otish

L a u r e n t i e n   P l a t e a u

St. John's

Prince Albert

Lake Winnipegosis

Akimiski I.

Anticosti I.

Charlottetown

askatoon

Lake Manitoba

Albany

Fort Albany

Quebec

St. Lawrence

Fredericton

Regina

Lake Winnipeg

Lake Nipigon

St John

Halifax

Winnipeg

Thunder Bay

Lake Superior

Montreal

Gulf of St. Lawrence

Ottawa

S T A T E S   O F   A M E R I C A

Lake Michigan

Georgian Bay

Lake Huron

Toronto

Lake Ontario

Missouri

Mississippi

Niagara Falls

Lake Erie

A T L A N T I C   O C E A N

0   500   1000   1500 Miles

0   500   1000   1500   2000 Km

Canada

Canada Land Use

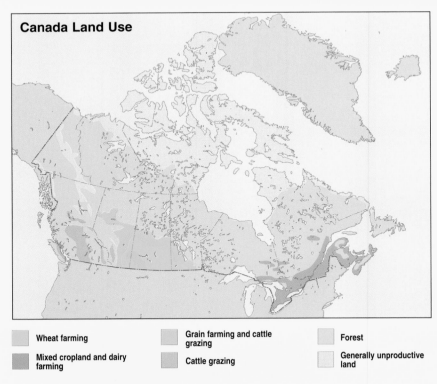

- ☐ Wheat farming
- ☐ Mixed cropland and dairy farming
- ☐ Grain farming and cattle grazing
- ☐ Cattle grazing
- ☐ Forest
- ☐ Generally unproductive land

Most Canadians are descended from European immigrants. First arrivals to the region were French settlers, who came in the 1760s, followed quickly by the Scots and later by the English and Irish in the 1800s. Europeans immigrated to Canada in great numbers following World War II, resulting in a population tracing its roots to Germany, Italy, Greece, Hungary, Ukraine, Poland, Norway, Sweden, and the Netherlands. Since then the bulk of immigrants has been from Southeast Asia. The largest non-English-speaking group is the French Canadians, who account for about 28 percent of the population. Nearly five million French Canadians live in French-speaking Québec. Another four million reside in the eastern half of the country. Some members of the **separatist** movement want an independent French-speaking Québec republic. Others simply want to preserve their French culture while remaining part of Canada. Native peoples of Canada account for about 2 percent of the population. Inuit claims to be properly recognized resulted in the new territory of Nunavut being formed in 1997.

Canada's mines produce a wide range of mineral ores, including iron, nickel, copper, zinc, molybdenum, uranium, gold, and platinum. The country also claims rich deposits of sulfur, asbestos, potash, and gypsum. These resources make Canada one of the world's largest mineral exporters. Hydroelectric power from the country's many large rivers, along with coal, oil, and natural gas, provide energy for homes and industry.

Much of Canada is forested, and the country is a major exporter of lumber (sawn wood), plywood, wood pulp, paper, and cardboard. The rich prairie soils of Alberta, Saskatchewan, and Manitoba produce most of Canada's wheat, oats, barley, and rye and feed crops for large herds of beef cattle. The eastern lowlands, with their milder climate, produce corn, vegetables, fruit, tobacco, and poultry and dairy products.

Lincoln Sea

500   1000   1500 Miles

0   500   1000   1500   2000 Km

G R E E N L A N D

ICELAND

Ellesmere I..

Greenland Sea

Devon I.

Baffin Bay

Davis Strait

Denmark Strait

Victoria I.

N U N A V U T

Baffin Island

Auyuittuo
N.P.

Foxe Basin

s I.

Baker Lake

Southampton
I.

Hudson Strait

nife

Dubawnt
Lake

Coats I.

Mansel I.

Feuilles

Nain

NEWFOUNDLAND
AND
LABRADOR

esolution

rt Smith

Lake
Athabasca

Churchill

Hudson Bay

Happy Valley-Goose Bay

Smallwood
Reservoir

A D A

Reindeer Lake

Nelson

Belcher Is.

La Grande

Gander

MANITOBA

Severn

James
Bay

Fort George

Q U É B E C

Anticosti I.

NEWFOUNDLAND
AND LABRADOR

St John's

Prince Albert

Lake
Winnipegosis

Lake
Winnipeg

ONTARIO

Akimiski
I.

Fort Albany

Peribonca

Gulf of St. Lawrence

PRINCE
EDWARD I.

Saskatoon

Albany

St. Lawrence

N E W
BRUNSWICK

Charlottetown

★ Regina

Riding Manitoba
Mountain
N.P.

Lake
Nipigon

Québec ★

Fredericton ●

NOVA
SCOTIA

KATCHEWAN

Winnipeg

Thunder Bay

Pukaskwa
N.P.

St John

★ Halifax

Lake Superior

Montréal

Georgian
Bay

Ottawa ●

ATLANTIC

ED S T A T E S   O F   A M E R I C A

Lake Michigan

Lake Huron

Toronto ●

Lake Ontario

OCEAN

Lake Erie

United States of America

United States of America

Status:	Federal Republic
Area:	3.53 million square miles
Population:	270 million
Capital:	Washington D.C.
Language:	English
Currency:	U.S. dollar (100 cents)

The United States forms the world's third-largest country by population and the fourth-largest by size. Only China and India have more people, and only Canada, China, and Russia have greater land areas. The United States occupies the entire central section of the North American continent, as well as Alaska in the far northwest and the Hawaiian Islands in the middle of the Pacific Ocean. A 5,500-mile border separates the United States from Canada, which is America's most important trading partner. In the south, Mexico and the United States share a 1,930-mile boundary. The U.S. Pacific coastline is 1,300 miles long. The East Coast runs for nearly 3,700 miles along the Atlantic Ocean and around the Gulf of Mexico.

The country's varied climate, fertile farmlands, and vast resources of timber minerals, **fossil fuels**, and water power make it one of the world's richest nations. In fact, some of its 50 states are like small countries in terms of their size, their population, and the amount of food and industrial goods they produce.

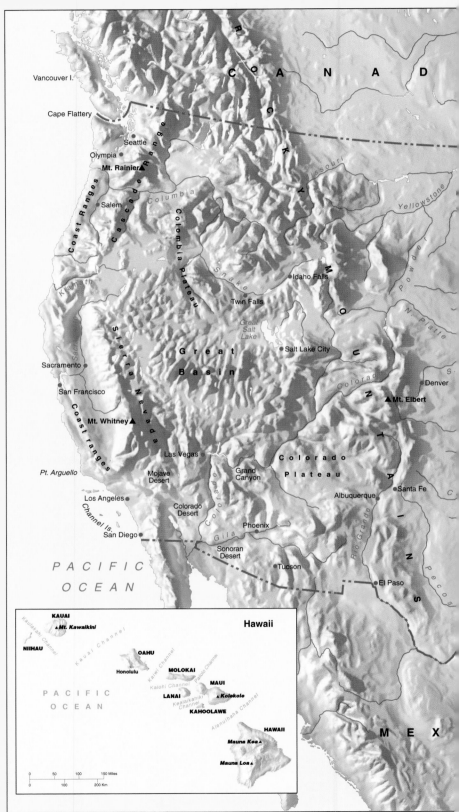

Alaska

CANADA

Gulf of St. Lawrence

Cape Sable

Red

Missouri

James

Lake Superior

Georgian Bay

Lake Huron

Lake Ontario

Lake Michigan

Niagara Falls

Connecticut

Boston
Cape Cod

Minneapolis

Mississippi

Grand Rapids

Detroit

Lake Erie

Hudson

Susquehanna

New York

Philadelphia

Sioux Falls

Madison

Chicago
Gary

Pittsburgh

Delaware Bay

Washington, D.C.★

UNITED STATES
OF AMERICA

Indianapolis Cincinnati

Ohio

James

Chesapeake Bay

Kansas City

Roanoke

Cape Hatteras

G r e a t

P l a i n s

kansas

imarron

White

Nashville

Tennessee

Cape Fear

Cape Fear

Oklahoma City

Arkansas

Memphis

Tombigbee

Chattahoochee

Atlanta Augusta

Savannah

A T L A N T I C

Red

Brazos

Colorado

Dallas

Trinity

Sabine

Red

Mississippi

Alabama

Altamaha

Savannah

O C E A N

Austin
Houston

San Antonio

Nueces

New Orleans

Mississippi Delta

Orlando Cape Canaveral

B A H A M A S

Rio Grande

GULF OF MEXICO

Lake Okeechobee

The Everglades

Grand
Bahama I.

Miami

Key West

Andros I.

Turks & Caicos
Is.

Florida Keys

Straits of Florida

CUBA

Great
Inagua I.

O

0		500 Miles	
0	500		1000 Km

United States of America

The United States is a federal republic, comprised of 50 states and the District of Columbia (D.C.)—where the country's government meets. In the federal system, the federal government makes decisions regarding foreign policy, defense, the justice system, health services, agricultural and industrial policy, and many aspects of taxation. These laws apply to the entire country. State and local governments discuss and regulate other issues such as education, public health, crime control, and local taxation.

Throughout its history, the United States has attracted immigrants from all over the world. The U.S. population mix is roughly 73 percent white—mainly of European origin—12 percent African American, 11 percent Hispanic, 3 percent Asian, and about 1 percent Native American. Nearly three-quarters of the population live in cities and towns.

Geology and climate have created a variety of natural resources. The West Coast—a region of forested mountains and fertile valleys—has a mild climate that is wet in the north and much drier in the south. Inland from the coast lie broad valleys and basins, rising to the rugged peaks of the Rocky Mountains. This basin and range area has few people but contains valuable minerals and is a vital mining and manufacturing area. Cattle graze in the north. To the south lie the deserts of Utah, Nevada, and California.

The Great Plains east of the Rockies have relatively little rainfall, but the rain they do receive falls mainly in summer, allowing these fertile plains to produce huge quantities of grain, meat, and dairy products. New England and the Atlantic states along the East Coast are famous for their historic sites and scenery but also have rich farmland and industrial centers such as Philadelphia, Buffalo, and Pittsburgh. The southern lowlands traditionally produce cotton, tobacco, and other warm-climate crops. The oil industry, manufacturing, and tourism are also essential to the economy of the south.

Alaska is the largest state in area and the smallest in number of people. Its population of 552,000 includes 85,000 Eskimo, Native Americans, and Aleuts. Almost two-thirds of Alaska's people live in the few large cities. The main industries are tourism, forestry, fishing, mining, and oil and gas.

Los Angeles, California, (*right*) is a thriving city with 3.5 million people in the city itself and another 3.5 million in the rest of Los Angeles County. Its richly varied population includes Hispanics, Asians, Pacific Islanders, and African Americans. The city is a major seaport, the home of the movie industry, and a center for the aviation and petroleum industries.

United States of America

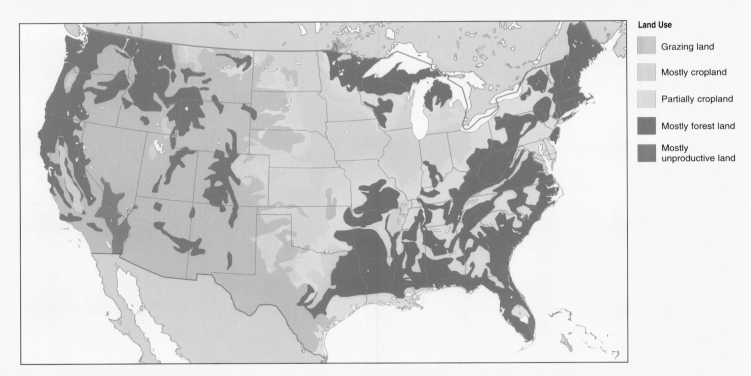

Land Use

- Grazing land
- Mostly cropland
- Partially cropland
- Mostly forest land
- Mostly unproductive land

Above: The United States is rich in natural resources. The fertile soils of the Midwest, the eastern states, and California produce cereal grains, vegetables, and fruit. Farmers in these areas also raise pigs, poultry, and dairy cattle. The drier western and southern grasslands produce prime beef. Forest lands yield both hardwood and softwood lumber, and the country has large deposits of coal, oil, gas, iron ore, copper, and other minerals. Compare the land use map (*above*) with the rainfall map (*below*). You can see at a glance what an important influence rainfall has on the way people use the land.

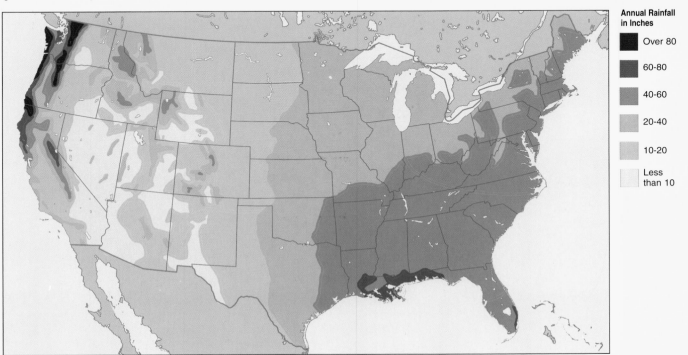

Annual Rainfall in Inches

- Over 80
- 60-80
- 40-60
- 20-40
- 10-20
- Less than 10

When the first European settlers arrived in North America during the early 1600s, the French settled mainly in the northeast in what would become Canada. The British traveled along the East Coast, and the Spanish stayed near the Gulf coast and settled the lands west of the Mississippi. By the 1750s, the population of these colonies had grown to almost 1.5 million. Life was difficult, but people eager to build a new future continued to arrive from Europe. Many were fleeing religious persecution. Some were adventurers. Others had no choice. Peoples from Africa were enslaved and shipped to North America, where they were sold to wealthy landowners as plantation workers and domestic servants.

By 1763, after winning the bitter Seven Years' War with France in Europe, Britain controlled most of eastern North America. By this time, however, the British colonies along the East Coast had become thriving, successful communities. The colonists resented British rule. The arguments grew bitter, eventually erupting in the American Revolution, which lasted from 1775 to 1783. At the war's end, the world had a new nation—the United States of America.

The United States continued to grow and prosper, gaining more territory from Britain, France, Spain, and Mexico. Farmers, ranchers, prospectors, and traders moved farther west, reaching the Pacific Coast by the mid-1800s. But America's troubles were not over. Between 1861 and 1865, the nation was torn, north to south, by the bitter struggle of the Civil War. In 1867 the United States bought the territory of Alaska from Russia, and it officially became the forty-ninth state in 1959. The Hawaiian Islands became the fiftieth state in the same year.

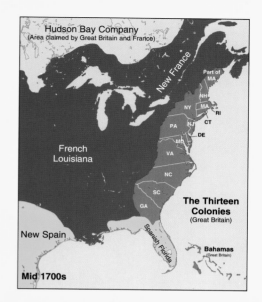

Top: By the mid-1700s, the 13 original British colonies lined the East Coast from Massachusetts to Georgia, with French territory to the north and west and Spanish territory to the south.

Center: The Treaty of Paris in 1783 ended the American Revolution. The United States gained territory stretching west to the Mississippi River. British territory was to the north, and Spanish colonial lands lay to the west and south.

Below Left: In 1803 President Thomas Jefferson almost doubled the size of the United States when he bought Louisiana from France, which had taken over the territory from Spain some years earlier.

Below Right: By the mid–1800s, the United States stretched all the way to the West Coast. Britain gave up its claim to Oregon in 1846, and huge areas were won from Mexico after the war of 1846–1848.

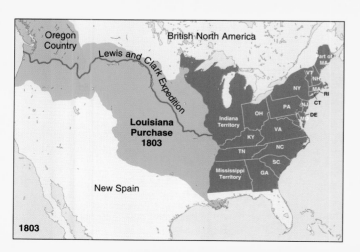

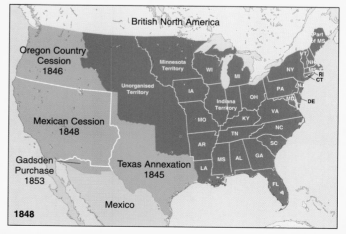

Mexico

Mexico

Status:	Federal Republic
Area:	736,946 square miles
Population:	97.5 million
Capital:	Mexico City
Language:	Spanish
Currency:	Mexican Peso (100 centavos)

Roughly one quarter of the Mexican people are farmers, and most of them work small farms in the highlands. Most of the country's wealth comes from its vast oil reserves and from minerals, textiles, forestry, and tourism.

Mexico has a variety of topographical features. North of the capital, Mexico City, the land is dominated by two north-south mountain ranges. The western Sierra Madre has peaks rising to 11,000 feet, and the eastern Sierra Madre reaches heights of more than 13,000 feet. Between the two ranges lies the Mexican Plateau. The northern part of the plateau is dry. It merges into the desert regions that stretch north and west to the U.S. border and the 760-mile-long desert peninsula of Baja (Lower) California. The plateau's southern section hosts a milder climate with more rain, and its rich volcanic soils support much of Mexico's fertile farmland.

A narrow coastal plain runs along the Pacific Coast. A wider plain, which snakes along the Gulf Coast and goes north of the seaport of Tampico, is covered with thorn bush and scrub. South of the city, the climate is more moist, and the vegetation becomes richer as it becomes part of the tropical rain forests of southeastern Mexico. The Yucatán Peninsula, a low limestone region, juts into the Gulf of Mexico. Dry scrubland covers the northern peninsula, but the southern end merges with the tropical forest claiming most of the narrow Isthmus of Tehuantepec.

More highlands dominate southern Mexico. To the south of Mexico City, a range of volcanic mountains cuts across the country. This range contains Mexico's highest peak—the 18,410 foot Pico de Orizaba—and many active volcanoes, including Iztaccíhuatl and Popocatepétl, both more than 17,000 feet above sea level. The Chiapas Highlands line the Pacific Coast in the far south, stretching into the Central American nations of Guatemala and El Salvador.

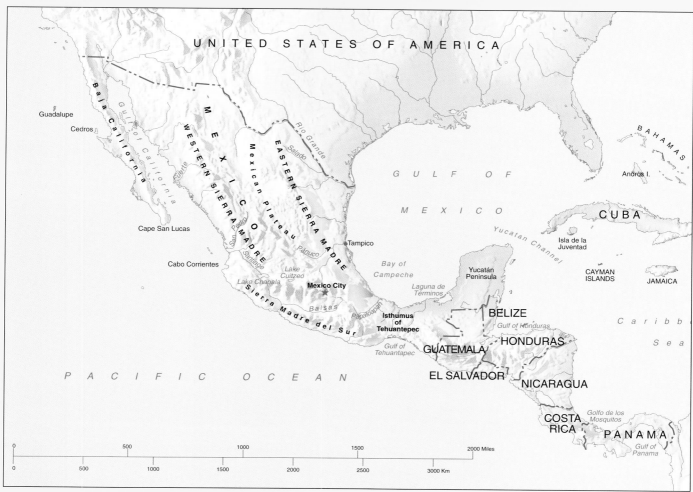

UNITED STATES OF AMERICA

Guadalupe

Cedros

Baja California

Gulf of California

M E X I C O

WESTERN SIERRA MADRE

WESTERN SIERRA MADRE

Mexican Plateau

EASTERN SIERRA MADRE

Rio Grande

Salado

GULF OF

MEXICO

B A H A M A S

Andros I.

Fuerte

San Pedro

Cape San Lucas

Cabo Corrientes

Santiago

Lake Cuitzeo

Lake Chapala

Panuco

Tampico

Bay of Campeche

Yucatán Channel

Isla de la Juventad

CUBA

CAYMAN ISLANDS

JAMAICA

Mexico City

Balsas

Sierra Madre del Sur

Papaloapan

Isthumus of Tehuantepec

Gulf of Tehuantepec

Laguna de Términos

Yucatán Peninsula

BELIZE

GUATEMALA

EL SALVADOR

Gulf of Honduras

HONDURAS

NICARAGUA

C a r i b b

S e a

P A C I F I C   O C E A N

COSTA RICA

Golfo de los Mosquitos

PANAMA

Gulf of Panama

| 0 | 500 | 1000 | 1500 | 2000 Miles |

| 0 | 500 | 1000 | 1500 | 2000 | 2500 | 3000 Km |

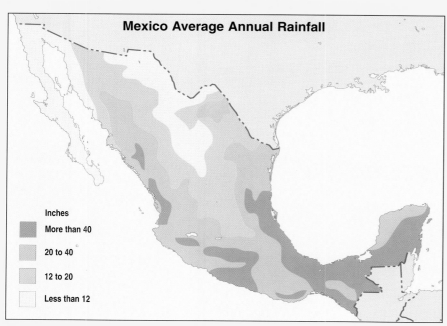

Mexico Average Annual Rainfall

Inches

More than 40

20 to 40

12 to 20

Less than 12

23

Mexico

Mexico has a long history. By 2000 B.C., large farming villages were dotting the southern highlands. Around 1000 B.C., Mexico had sizable towns, with elaborate temples and stone carvings. And by 400 B.C., the Olmec Indians had invented the calendar and systems for writing and counting. The great empires of the Mayan, Olmec, Mixtec, Toltec, and Aztec peoples flourished for centuries. In A.D.1521, Spanish soldiers conquered the Aztecs. For the next 300 years, Spain ruled the country as one of its colonies. In fact, most modern Mexicans are **mestizos**—people who have both Indian and European ancestors.

Mexico gained its independence from Spain in 1821, but a century of wars and unrest followed. Successive governments have introduced land reforms and have encouraged industry, but the country still struggles with a weak economy, high unemployment, and a growing population. The birthrate is very high, and more than half the people are less than 20 years old. Poverty troubles both rural and urban areas. Mexico City has a population of more than 15 million, and five other cities have more than a million people.

Roughly one-fourth of Mexico's people make their living from farming, mainly in the southern part of the plateau and in the valleys of the south. The northern regions are so dry that farmers must irrigate their crops. The primary agricultural products are corn, wheat, coffee, cotton, and a wide variety of fruits and vegetables. Beef cattle, sheep, and goats graze in the north. Dairy cows thrive mostly in the south where the pasture is better. The eastern Sierra Madre contains rich deposits of coal and iron ore, and Monterrey is home to the iron and steel industry. Other manufacturing centers include Mexico City, Guadalajara, Chihuahua, Mexicali, Puebla, Tijuana, and Veracruz. Workers produce cars, foods, beverages, chemicals, petroleum products, cement, and fertilizers. New factories built near the U.S. border manufacture car components and electrical goods for the United States. The oil industry operates from platforms in the Gulf.

Above: Mexico has hundreds of ancient monuments, such as this Mayan pyramid, and many colorful local traditions.

Below: Veracruz, on the Gulf of Mexico, is the country's main port. It was founded in 1519 by Hernán Cortés.

24

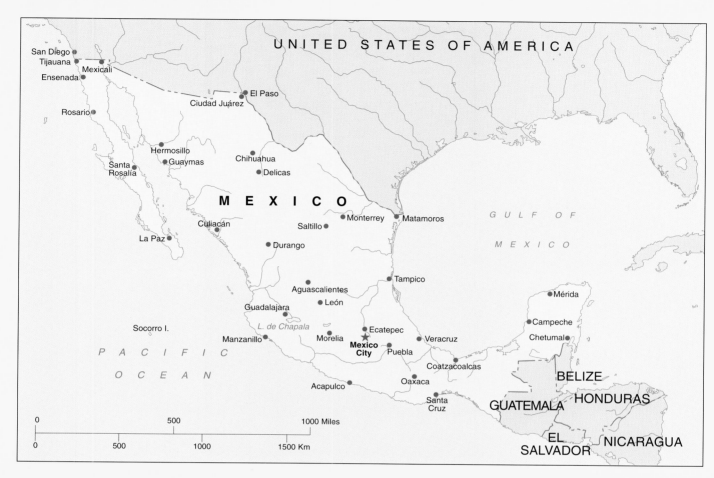

UNITED STATES OF AMERICA

San Diego
Tijuana
Mexicali
Ensenada

Rosario

El Paso
Ciudad Juárez

Hermosillo
Santa
Rosalía
Guaymas

Chihuahua
Delicas

M E X I C O

Culiacán
La Paz

Saltillo
Monterrey
Matamoros

GULF OF

MEXICO

Durango

Tampico

Aguascalientes
León

Mérida

Guadalajara

L. de Chapala

Campeche

Socorro I.

Manzanillo
Morelia
Ecatepec
Mexico City
Puebla
Veracruz

Chetumal

P A C I F I C

O C E A N

Acapulco

Coatzacoalcas

Oaxaca

BELIZE

Santa
Cruz

GUATEMALA

HONDURAS

EL
SALVADOR

NICARAGUA

0		500		1000 Miles

0	500	1000	1500 Km

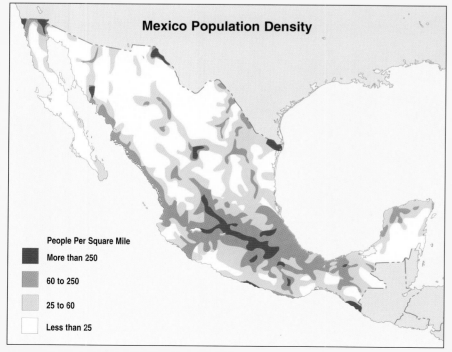

Mexico Population Density

People Per Square Mile

More than 250

60 to 250

25 to 60

Less than 25

Despite improvements in fuel quality and vehicle emission standards, Mexico City's three million automobiles and thousands of trucks and buses make it still one of the world's most polluted cities.

Bermuda, Bahamas, Turks and Caicos Islands

Bermuda

Status:	Self-governing British Crown Colony
Area:	21 square miles
Population:	65,000
Capital:	Hamilton
Language:	English
Currency:	Bermudan dollar (100 cents)

Turks and Caicos Islands

Status:	British Dependency
Area:	166 square miles
Population:	13,000
Capital:	Cockburn Town
Language:	English
Currency:	U.S. dollar (100 cents)

The Turks and Caicos group contains about 30 small islands located at the southeastern edge of the Grand Bahama Bank. Eight of the islands are inhabited, and the people earn their living from tourism and banking. Grand Turk, the largest island, houses an important U.S. missile tracking station. Both France and Spain once claimed the islands, which Britain has governed since 1766.

Bermuda is a cluster of more than 300 small islands, 580 miles off Cape Hatteras, North Carolina. Most of the islands are tiny. Only 20 of them are inhabited, and the largest, Great Bermuda, is linked by bridges and causeways to the five other main islands. The islands are made of limestone—the remains of ancient **coral reefs**—and they are still surrounded by living reefs. The warm, mild climate, sandy beaches, pastel-colored buildings, and profusion of wildflowers attract more than 500,000 visitors each year. Tourism is the main industry, along with banking and insurance. The islands have no rivers or lakes, so rainwater is collected from roofs and stored in underground tanks. There are a few small farms, but most of the islands' food supplies are imported.

Left: Hamilton is the capital and chief port of Bermuda. It is a popular tourist resort, and cruise ships can tie up right alongside the city's main street, Front Street. Pastel-painted buildings and sunshades for the traffic police all add to the city's charm.

Below: Golden beaches and subtropical vegetation make the Bahamas a vacationers' paradise.

Bahamas

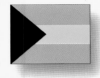

Status:	Independent Nation
Area:	5,365 square miles
Population:	300,000
Capital:	Nassau
Languages:	English, Creole
Currency:	Bahamian dollar (100 cents)

The Bahamas consist of 27 inhabited islands and nearly 3,000 uninhabited small islands and cays. These small landforms are scattered across 90,000 square miles of limestone and coral reefs known as the Grand Bahama Bank in the western Atlantic. The islands nearest the U.S. mainland lie 60 miles off the Florida coast, while the southernmost islands in the archipelago are just 50 miles from the Caribbean island of Cuba. The Bahamas enjoy a subtropical climate, and the economy is based on tourism, sport fishing, gambling, and banking. Many historians believe that Columbus's first landfall in 1492 was on the Bahamian island of San Salvador.

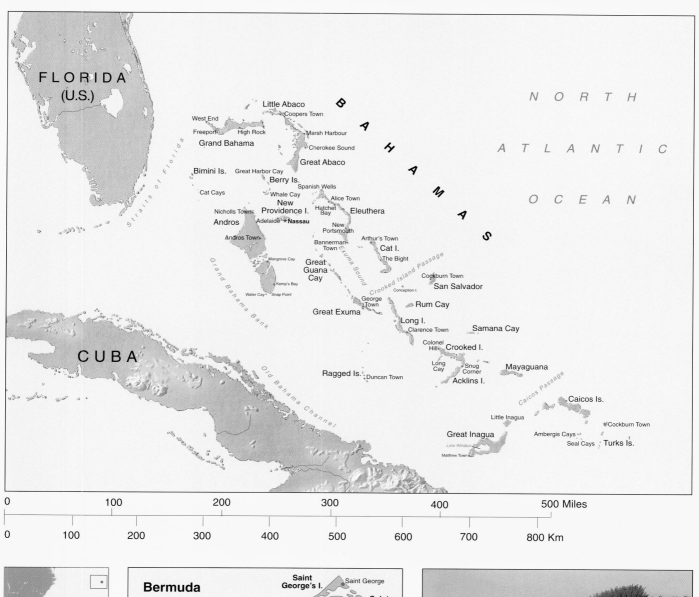

FLORIDA
(U.S.)

B A H A M A S

N O R T H

A T L A N T I C

O C E A N

Little Abaco
West End
Coopers Town
Freeport High Rock
Marsh Harbour
Grand Bahama
Cherokee Sound
Great Abaco
Bimini Is.
Great Harbor Cay
Berry Is.
Spanish Wells
Cat Cays
Whale Cay
Alice Town
Nicholls Town
New
Providence I.
Hatchet
Bay
Eleuthera
Andros
Adelaide ★Nassau
New
Portsmouth
Andros Town
Arthur's Town
Bannerman
Town
Cat I.
Mangrove Cay
The Bight
Great
Guana
Cay
Cockburn Town
Kemp's Bay
Conception I.
San Salvador
Water Cay Snap Point
George
Town
Rum Cay
Great Exuma
Long I.
Samana Cay
Clarence Town
Colonel
Hill
Crooked I.
Long
Cay
Mayaguana
Ragged Is. Duncan Town
Snug
Corner
Acklins I.

Straits of Florida

Grand Bahama Bank

CUBA

Old Bahama Channel

Exuma Sound

Crooked Island Passage

Caicos Passage

Caicos Is.
Little Inagua
Cockburn Town
Great Inagua
Ambergis Cays
Lake Windsor
Seal Cays Turks Is.
Matthew Town

0	100	200	300	400	500 Miles

0	100	200	300	400	500	600	700	800 Km

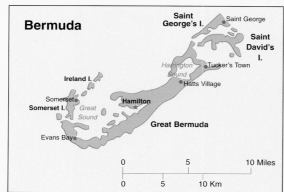

Bermuda

Saint
George's I.
Saint George
Saint
David's
I.
Tucker's Town
Harrington
Sound
Ireland I.
Hatts Village
Somerset
Hamilton
Somerset I.
Great
Sound
Great Bermuda
Evans Bay

0	5	10 Miles

0	5	10 Km

Right: Bermuda's financial services and generous tax laws make the islands a popular base for international businesses and wealthy individuals as well as a major tourist destination.

27

Cuba

Cuba

Status:	Socialist Republic
Area:	42,402 square miles
Population:	11.1 million
Capital:	Havana
Language:	Spanish
Currency:	Cuban peso (100 centavos)

Cuba lies 90 miles south of the tip of Florida. The largest of the Caribbean islands, Cuba is 120 miles wide and more than 750 miles long. The landscape is varied with high mountains to the west, middle, and east. Nearly three-quarters of the land consist of low rolling hills, fertile valleys, and broad plains. Cuba's climate is subtropical, with a warm dry season lasting from November to April and a mild rainy season occurring from May to October. Hurricanes frequently hit the island in the second half of the rainy season, often causing great damage to crops and buildings.

Spain ruled Cuba for nearly 400 years, but the island gained its independence in 1898. Decades of political troubles followed. For 12 years, the country had a democratic government that Fulgencio Batista overthrew in 1952. He, in turn, was ousted by Fidel Castro in 1959. President Castro's Communist government took control of the island's industries and most of the farmland. Under the Communist regime, education and health improved. Roughly 94 percent of the population can read and write, and life expectancy is 75 years.

Tobacco and coffee are grown on the higher ground, along with Cuba's main crop, sugarcane, which domin-ates more than half of all the cultivated land and accounts for nearly 80 percent of the island's exports. Bananas, citrus fruits, rice, tomatoes, and a wide variety of vegetables thrive on the fertile lower ground, and beef and dairy cattle graze on the rich grasslands. Fishing is another state-run industry. In addition to chromium, iron, manganese, copper, and silver, Cuba has one of the world's largest deposits of nickel. The country exports these minerals in great quantities and manufactures cement and fertilizers for export. Cuba's factories produce farm tools, paper, rum, textiles, and cigars.

Above right: Royal palms dot the sugar-cane fields of the "Valley of the Sugarmills" near the old town of Trinidad on the island of Cuba.

Right: Small farms on Cuba grow tobacco, sugarcane, and fruit and sell all their produce to the government.

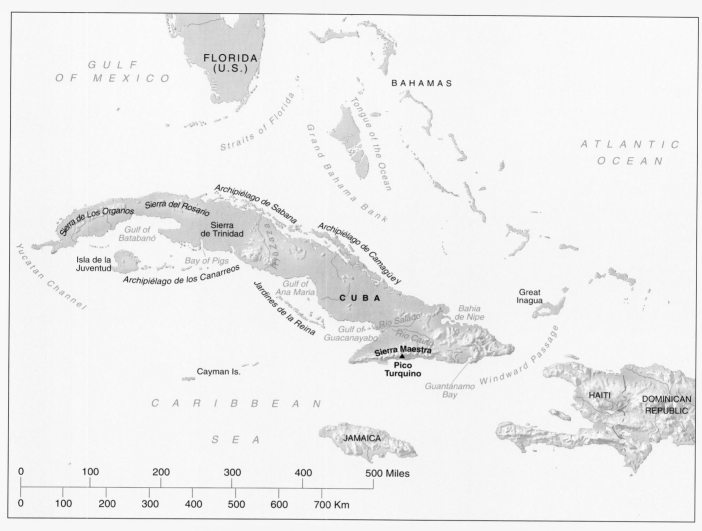

GULF
OF MEXICO

FLORIDA
(U.S.)

BAHAMAS

Straits of Florida

Tongue of the Ocean

Grand Bahama Bank

ATLANTIC
OCEAN

Sierra de Los Organos

Sierra del Rosario

Archipiélago de Sabana

Gulf of
Batabanó

Sierra
de Trinidad

Archipiélago de Camagüey

Yucatan Channel

Isla de la
Juventud

Bay of Pigs

Archipiélago de los Canarreos

Zaza

Gulf of
Ana Maria

C U B A

Great
Inagua

Jardines de la Reina

Gulf of
Guacanayabo

Río Salado

Río Cauto

Bahía
de Nipe

Sierra Maestra ▲
Pico
Turquino

Guantánamo
Bay

Windward Passage

Cayman Is.

C A R I B B E A N

S E A

JAMAICA

HAITI

DOMINICAN
REPUBLIC

| 0 | 100 | 200 | 300 | 400 | 500 Miles |

| 0 | 100 | 200 | 300 | 400 | 500 | 600 | 700 Km |

Havana
Matanzas

Marianao
Cárdenas

Artemisa
Sagua la Grande

Colón
Santa
Clara

Pinar del Río
Aguada
de Pasajeros
Caibarién

Guane
Cienfuegos

Nueva
Gerona
Sancti-Spíritus

Trinidad

Santa Fé
Florida

Isla de la
Juventud
Camagüey

Yucatan Channel
C U B A
Banes

Jardines de la Reine
Holguín

Manzanillo
Baracoa

Cayman Islands
Guantánamo
Santiago
de Cuba

| 0 | 100 | 200 | 300 miles |

| 0 | 100 | 200 | 300 | 400 Km |

Jamaica and the Cayman Islands

Jamaica

Status:	Constitutional Monarchy
Area:	4,181 square miles
Population:	2.6 million
Capital:	Kingston
Languages:	English, Creole, Hindi, Spanish, Chinese
Currency:	Jamaican dollar (100 cents)

Cayman Islands

Status:	British Dependency
Area:	100 square miles
Population:	29,000
Capital:	Georgetown
Language:	English
Currency:	Cayman dollar (100 cents)

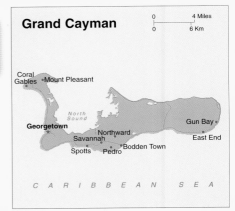

The third-largest of the Caribbean islands (after Cuba and Hispaniola), Jamaica is located about 100 miles south of the eastern end of Cuba. The 145-mile-long, 50-mile-wide island is mountainous, with Blue Mountain Peak rising to 7,400 feet above sea level near its eastern end. Moisture-bearing winds blowing from the west carry up to 200 inches of rain a year to the highlands, most of it falling between May and October. Jamaica's lowlands are drier, with an average of 80 inches a year.

Jamaicans are an interesting mix of people. Most are of African descent, but others are descended from British, Portuguese, Spanish, German, Indian, and Chinese immigrants. Claimed by Christopher Columbus in 1494, Jamaica was ruled by Spain until 1655, when Britain took control.

Thin soils on top of limestone make farming difficult, but sugarcane, fruits, coffee, cacao beans, and spices do well in the fertile valleys and coastal plains. Jamaica exports much of its produce, mainly from the cities of Kingston and Montego Bay. Most of the island's income derives from tourism and from mining and exporting bauxite—the principal ore of aluminum and of alumina.

Columbus claimed the three tiny Cayman Islands for Spain in 1503, but they have been governed by Britain since 1670. About 75 percent of the people are of African descent. The rest are mainly British and American. The islands are made of limestone and are fringed by coral reefs. Temperatures range from 55°F to 95°F, and rainfall is low at around 56 inches annually. The islands support a small fishing industry, and farmers raise tomatoes, bananas, pigs, cows, and poultry. The Cayman Islands' principal businesses are finance and tourism. Very liberal tax laws have attracted the headquarters of nearly 18,000 companies and more than 400 banks. Luxury tourism and the world's most expensive beachfront real estate provide 70 percent of the islands' total income.

Below: Jamaica is one of the world's leading producers of bauxite, shown here, the mineral ore from which aluminum is made. The country's mines also produce gypsum, which is used to make plasterboard and other construction materials.

Little Cayman
CAYMAN ISLANDS
Cayman Brac
Grand Cayman

CARIBBEAN SEA

G R E A T E R   A N T I L L E S

C U B A

Montego Bay
JAMAICA
Blue Mountain Peak ▲
May Pen
Kingston

Jamaica Channel

HAITI

0   120 Miles
0   240 Km

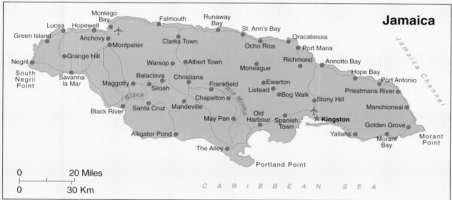

Jamaica

Montego Bay
Lucea
Hopewell
Green Island
Anchovy
Montpelier
Grange Hill
Negril
South Negril Point
Savanna la Mar
Maggotty
Balaclava
Siloah
Black River
Santa Cruz
Mandeville
Alligator Pond
The Alley
Warsop
Albert Town
Christiana
Frankfield
Chapelton
May Pen
Old Harbour
Clarks Town
Falmouth
Runaway Bay
St. Ann's Bay
Ocho Rios
Moneague
Listead
Ewarton
Bog Walk
Spanish Town
Portland Point
Oracabessa
Port Maria
Richmond
Annotto Bay
Hope Bay
Port Antonio
Priestmans River
Stony Hill
Kingston
Golden Grove
Yallahs
Manchioneal
Morant Bay
Morant Point

Black River
Rio Minho

Jamaica Channel

0   20 Miles
0   30 Km

C A R I B B E A N   S E A

Below left: Sugarcane is the main ingredient of rum, one of Jamaica's famous exports.

Below: Some stretches of the coast are a tourist's paradise, while others provide loading points for the bauxite carriers.

31

Haiti and the Dominican Republic

Haiti

Status:	Republic
Area:	10,641 square miles
Population:	7.5 million
Capital:	Port-au-Prince
Languages:	French, Creole
Currency:	Gourde (100 centimes)

Haiti makes up the westernmost one-third of the island of Hispaniola, the second-largest island in the Caribbean. Haiti is a mountainous nation, with very little farmland and few natural resources. It is also heavily populated and, as a result, is one of the poorest countries in the world. Almost two-thirds of the people just manage to make a living on small farms in the valleys and on steep hillsides or by fishing along the coast.

From 1697 until 1804, France ruled Haiti. The country gained its independence after a slave revolt, giving Haiti the distinction of being the world's oldest black republic. Nearly 200 years of turmoil followed. Among the worst periods was the brutal father-son regime of François and Jean-Claude Duvalier. It lasted from 1957 to 1986. In 1990 the first democratically elected president, Jean-Bertrand Aristide, took office but seven months later was forced into exile by supporters of the old regime. In 1994 the United States sent troops to restore democracy and to return Aristide to power. Haiti's later governments have continued to struggle for stability.

Big hydroelectric projects can sometimes be environmental disasters. When this dam was built at Pelgré in Haiti, the surrounding forests were cut down. With no trees to protect them, the hillside soils were soon washed away by the heavy rains, and the reservoir was clogged with silt.

Dominican Republic

Status:	Republic
Area:	18,680 square miles
Population:	8.3 million
Capital:	Santo Domingo
Language:	Spanish
Currency:	Dominican Peso (100 centavos)

The Dominican Republic has fared much better than its neighbor on Hispaniola. The land is dominated by mountains, including the highest peak in the Caribbean, the 10,414 foot Duarte Peak. But the country also has fertile valleys, lowlands, and coastal plains. The climate is tropical, with average temperatures around 77°F, and ample rainfall, especially in the summer.

The Dominican Republic produces sugarcane, coffee, rice, and tobacco, as well as cacao beans, fruits, and vegetables. In rural areas, most people farm small holdings, producing enough for their families and a small surplus to sell in the local markets. In the lowland areas, privately owned estates employ large numbers of workers in the sugarcane fields and coffee and cacao plantations. Mineral exports include bauxite, nickel, silver, and gold. The Dominican Republic is also developing its tourist industry by building resorts along the northern coast. Visitors increased from 5,000 to 65,000 between 1987 and 1990, and numbers continue to rise. Most of the tourists are from Canada, the United States, and Europe.

Opposite: Troops patrol the streets in Haiti after a disturbance. Political unrest is common in countries where a few people hold most of the wealth, while the rest struggle to survive in poor housing, with not enough food or adequate medical services.

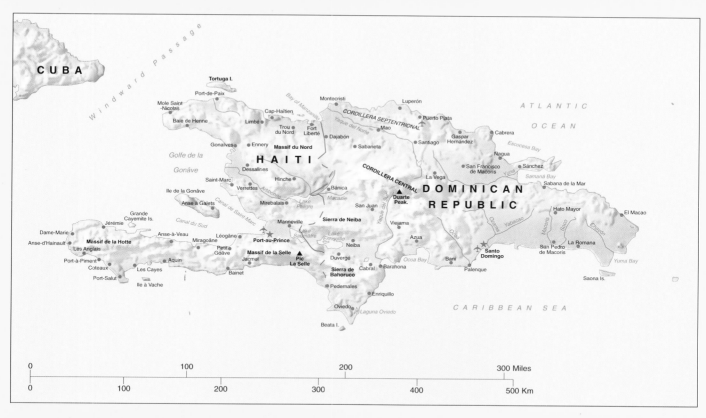

Puerto Rico

Puerto Rico

Status:	Self-governing U.S. Commonwealth
Area:	3,421 square miles
Population:	3.9 million
Capital:	San Juan
Languages:	Spanish, English
Currency:	U.S. dollar (100 cents)

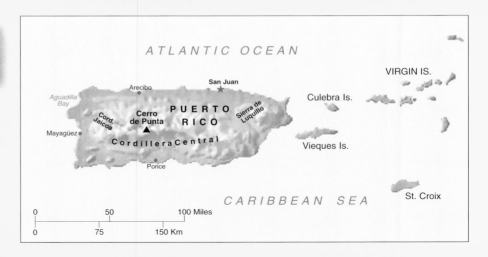

Puerto Rico is about 100 miles long and 35 miles wide. It is mountainous, with a narrow coastal plain, so agricultural land is scarce. The best land is used for growing sugarcane, coffee, bananas, tobacco, tropical fruits, and spices. The climate is tropical, creating good growing conditions on the moist northeastern side of the island, but the island lies in the track of Atlantic hurricanes and often suffers devastating storms.

Since a referendum (a public vote) in 1952, Puerto Rico has been a self-governing commonwealth of the United States. The island creates its own laws, as long as they don't conflict with those of the United States, and its people can travel freely to the mainland. Puerto Ricans can vote in U.S. presidential primaries but not in the actual elections. The government of Puerto Rico is based on that of the United States, with a Senate, a House of Representatives, and a president who is elected every four years. Health and education have improved faster than anywhere else in the Caribbean. Free medical and dental care is available to everyone, life expectancy has increased from 46 years to 74, and 90 percent of the population can read and write.

Compared to most other Caribbean islands, Puerto Rico is heavily industrialized, and a large proportion of the people make their homes in urban areas. Nearly half the population lives in or around the capital, San Juan, working in factories that produce textiles, clothing, electrical goods, leather goods, and processed foods. More than 85 percent of the country's exports and 65 percent of its imports are with the United States. Other major employers are the huge petroleum refinery and chemical works on the southwestern coast; the mining and smelting of copper; and the growing tourist industry.

Above: An aerial view shows one of the large rum distilleries in San Juan, Puerto Rico. Rum—made from sugarcane—is one of the traditional exports of the Caribbean.

Right: Puerto Rico's lowlands are mainly farmed, but the inland areas still contain large tracts of untouched tropical rain forest.

Below: Puerto Rico has one of the fastest-growing economies in the Caribbean. The country's success is shown by the modern buildings in Hato Rey—San Juan's financial district.

Leeward Islands

The Leeward Islands form the northern section of the long island arc known as the Lesser Antilles, which stretches from just east of Puerto Rico to the coast of South America. The Leeward Islands extend from the Virgin Islands to Guadeloupe, while the Windward Islands continue the island chain almost to the coast of Venezuela. The Leeward and Windward Islands are the tops of a chain of submarine volcanoes that mark the line on the seabed where two sections of the earth's rocky crust meet. They form a natural breakwater of islands and coral reefs separating the Caribbean Sea from the Atlantic Ocean.

The Leeward group contains about 15 main islands and hundreds of small islets. It totals roughly 1,500 square miles and is home to about 700,000 people. Arawak and Carib Indians were the original inhabitants, but immigration and exploration resulted in a mixed population—descendants of Europeans, Africans brought in as slaves, Indian workers, and settlers from Asia and North and South America. The Leeward Islands contain two independent countries, as well as several dependencies of the United States, Britain, France, and the Netherlands.

The islands have warm, dry, tropical climates, with temperatures around 80°F for most of the year and total annual rainfall of 30 to 40 inches. Local farmers grow tobacco, cotton, sugarcane, and a wide variety of fruits and vegetables. Tourism is essential to most of the islands' economies. The beautiful scenery, colonial architecture, sandy beaches, clear water, and opportunities for leisure activities attract thousands of international visitors.

Tourism is the basis of Antigua's economy, with beautiful white sand beaches and a warm sunny climate drawing tourists from all over the world.

UNITED STATES OF AMERICA

GULF OF MEXICO

Yucatan Channel

Campeche Bay

MEXICO

BELIZE

Gulf of Honduras

Gulf of Tehuantepec

GUATEMALA

HONDURAS

EL SALVADOR

NICARAGUA

PACIFIC OCEAN

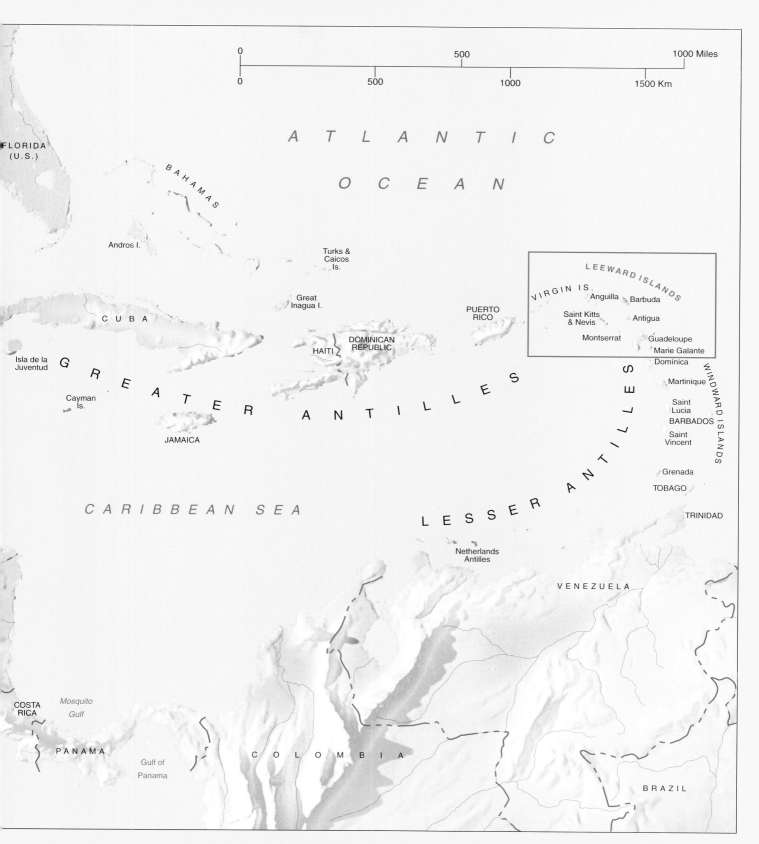

ATLANTIC

OCEAN

FLORIDA
(U.S.)

BAHAMAS

Andros I.

Turks &
Caicos
Is.

Great
Inagua I.

PUERTO
RICO

LEEWARD ISLANDS

VIRGIN IS.

Anguilla   Barbuda

CUBA

Saint Kitts
& Nevis

Antigua

DOMINICAN
REPUBLIC

Guadeloupe

HAITI

Montserrat

Marie Galante

Isla de la
Juventud

G R E A T E R   A N T I L L E S

Domínica

WINDWARD ISLANDS

Martinique

Cayman
Is.

Saint
Lucia

BARBADOS

JAMAICA

Saint
Vincent

L E S S E R   A N T I L L E S

Grenada

TOBAGO

CARIBBEAN   SEA

TRINIDAD

Netherlands
Antilles

VENEZUELA

COSTA
RICA

Mosquito
Gulf

PANAMA

Gulf of
Panama

C O L O M B I A

BRAZIL

Leeward Islands

U.S. Virgin Islands

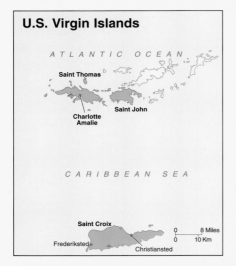

British Virgin Islands

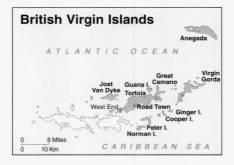

Barbuda / Antigua

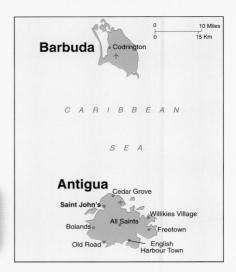

British Virgin Islands

Status:	British Dependency
Area:	59 square miles
Population:	18,000
Capital:	Road Town (on Tortola)
Language:	English
Currency:	U.S. dollar (100 cents)

U.S. Virgin Islands

Status:	Self-governing U.S. Territory
Area:	130 square miles
Population:	102,000
Capital:	Charlotte Amalie (on Saint Thomas)
Language:	English
Currency:	U.S. dollar (100 cents)

Antigua and Barbuda

Status:	Constitutional Monarchy
Area:	170 square miles
Population:	100,000
Capital:	Saint John's (on Antigua)
Language:	English
Currency:	Eastern Caribbean dollar (100 cents)

British Virgin Islands

This British island group contains 4 main islands and 36 smaller ones. About 75 percent of the people live on the largest island, Tortola. The islands receive more than 325,000 visitors each year and are a popular tax haven. Rum is the main export.

U.S. Virgin Islands

Most of the population of this island group lives on the largest islands—Saint Thomas, Saint Croix, and Saint John— but the territory also covers 65 smaller islands. Residents are U.S. citizens. Tourism is the primary industry, but Saint Croix also has oil refineries and bauxite processing plants.

Antigua and Barbuda

Antigua is hilly and rugged, made of volcanic rocks that create good soils in the valleys and lowlands. Barbuda is a low, mainly wooded coral island. Tourism is important, in addition to fishing (especially for lobster), market gardening, and Sea Island cotton production.

Left: The cable car at Charlotte Amalie on the island of Saint Thomas in the U.S. Virgin Islands provides a spectacular view of the bay, dotted with yachts and visiting cruise ships.

Far Left: The town of Charlotte Amalie on the island of Saint Thomas

Saint Kitts and Nevis

Status:	Constitutional Monarchy
Area:	139 square miles
Population:	40,000
Capital:	Basseterre
Language:	English
Currency:	Eastern Caribbean dollar (100 cents)

Saint Kitts and Nevis

These twin volcanic islands feature peaks of more than 3,000 feet above sea level that are covered with lush tropical rain forests. The lowlands are fertile and are used mainly for growing sugarcane, cotton, and tropical fruits. Tourism is the biggest industry, but the islands also produce textiles, leather, and electronic goods.

Montserrat

Status:	British Dependency
Area:	40 square miles
Population:	12,500
Capital:	Plymouth
Language:	English
Currency:	Eastern Caribbean dollar (100 cents)

Montserrat

Rugged and hilly with dense forests, Montserrat is famous for its volcanic eruptions. Volcanic rocks provide fertile soils and dark-colored sandy beaches. Tourism supplies one-quarter of the island's income, but Montserrat also exports Sea Island cotton, tropical fruits and vegetables, and manufactured electrical goods.

Anguilla

Status:	British Dependency
Area:	37 square miles
Population:	8,900
Capital:	The Valley
Languages:	English, Creole
Currency:	Eastern Caribbean dollar (100 cents)

Anguilla

This long, thin coral island is very flat—rising only to 200 feet above sea level. Low rainfall and poor soil hamper farming. The main crops are peas, beans, corn, and sweet potatoes. Anguilla's economy relies mostly on tourism and on exporting lobsters. Many of the island's most beautiful reefs have been damaged by removing coral to sell as tourist souvenirs.

Guadeloupe

Status:	Overseas Department of France
Area:	653 square miles
Population:	400,000
Capital:	Basse-Terre
Language:	French
Currency:	French franc (100 centimes)

Guadeloupe

Guadeloupe is a group of eight islands, the two largest being mountainous and volcanic Basse-Terre and lower Grand-Terre. The islands export sugar, bananas, and rum but depend heavily on aid from France.

Windward Islands and Barbados

From north to south, Dominica, Martinique, Saint Lucia, Saint Vincent and the Grenadines, and Grenada make up the Windward Island group. Barbados, lying about 40 miles to the east, is considered a separate island because it is not geologically connected to the Windward Island chain. Total land area of the Windward Islands is approximately 1,000 square miles, and the population numbers roughly 720,000.

Like the Leeward Islands to the north, Arawak Indians originally inhabited the Windward group, which Europeans (mainly British and French) settled on in the early 1600s. Martinique has remained a French possession, while the other territories became British colonies and later gained their independence. Years of migration has resulted in a population of mainly African descent, with small numbers of immigrants from Europe and North and South America.

Some of the smaller islands are composed of limestone and coral and therefore have very thin and infertile soils. These islands rely mainly on tourism. The larger islands are volcanic, and their mountainous interiors are covered in dense forests. The volcanic rocks produce rich soils that collect in the valleys and coastal plains, providing good farmland. Primary agricultural products are bananas, cacao beans, sugarcane, arrowroot, nutmeg, and mace. A few of the islands have small industries, but tourism is generally the most important source of income.

Small-scale fishing in the shallow coastal waters is a traditional way of life in Grenada. These fishing crews will sell most of their catch in the local market.

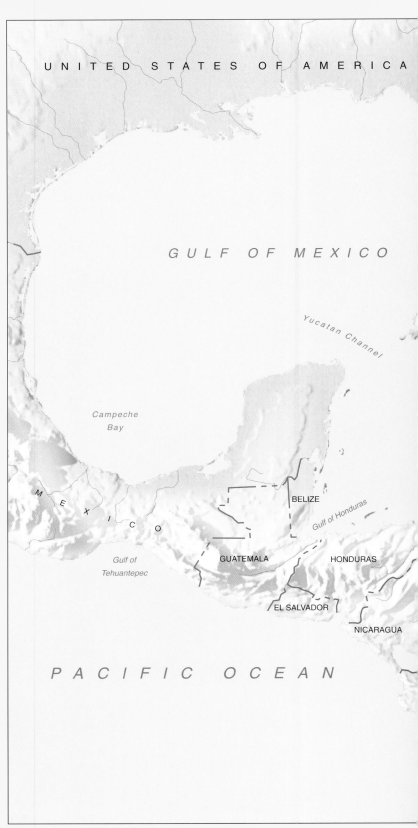

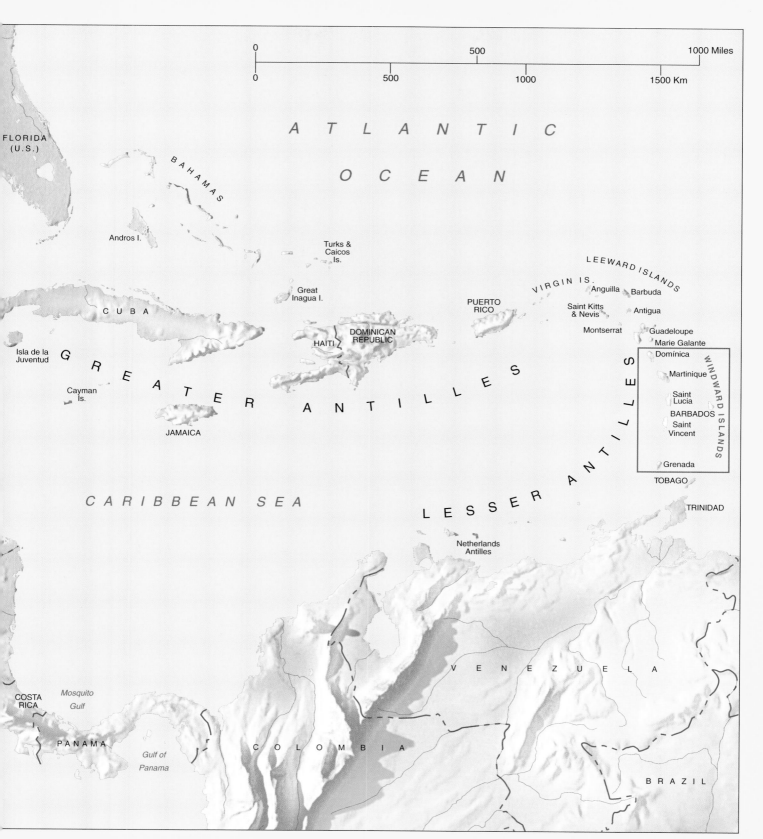

0   500   1000 Miles

0   500   1000   1500 Km

A T L A N T I C

O C E A N

FLORIDA
(U.S.)

B A H A M A S

Andros I.

Turks &
Caicos
Is.

LEEWARD ISLANDS

Great
Inagua I.

VIRGIN IS.

Anguilla   Barbuda

PUERTO
RICO

Saint Kitts
& Nevis

Antigua

C U B A

DOMINICAN
REPUBLIC

Montserrat

Guadeloupe

HAITI

Marie Galante

Isla de la
Juventud

Dominica

G R E A T E R

Martinique

WINDWARD ISLANDS

Cayman
Is.

A N T I L L E S

Saint
Lucia

BARBADOS

Saint
Vincent

JAMAICA

Grenada

TOBAGO

C A R I B B E A N   S E A

L E S S E R   A N T I L L E S

TRINIDAD

Netherlands
Antilles

V E N E Z U E L A

COSTA
RICA

*Mosquito
Gulf*

P A N A M A

*Gulf of
Panama*

C O L O M B I A

B R A Z I L

Windward Islands and Barbados

Dominica

Status:	Republic
Area:	290 square miles
Population:	100,000
Capital:	Roseau
Languages:	English, French patois
Currency:	Eastern Caribbean dollar (100 cents)

Dominica

The island is mountainous, volcanic, and densely forested. Its climate is hot, averaging 80°F, and wet, with 70 inches of rain falling annually on the coast and well over 200 inches blanketing the hills. A small tourist industry exists, but the islanders primarily support themselves by exporting bananas, coconuts, oranges, and grapefruits—mainly to the United States and Britain.

Martinique

Status:	Overseas Department of France
Area:	409 square miles
Population:	400,000
Capital:	Fort-de-France
Languages:	French, Creole
Currency:	French franc (100 centimes)

Martinique

Martinique's highest peak is the volcano Mont Pelée (4,583 feet above sea level), which erupted in 1902, engulfing the town of Saint-Pierre and killing 30,000 people. Farmers grow tropical fruits for export and vegetables for local use. Other islanders work in tourism and in the oil refineries, rum distilleries, and sugar-processing factories.

Saint Lucia

Status:	Constitutional Monarchy
Area:	236 square miles
Population:	150,000
Capital:	Castries
Languages:	English, French patois
Currency:	Eastern Caribbean dollar (100 cents)

Saint Lucia

Saint Lucia is mountainous, with dense forests and deep, fertile valleys. About one-third of its people work in agriculture—producing bananas, cacao beans, and copra for export. Light industries operate in the **free-trade zone** at Vieux Fort, a deepwater port for transferring oil between tankers. Cruise ships dock at the modern harbor of the city of Castries.

Left: Pineapples thrive on a big plantation in Martinique.

Saint Vincent and the Grenadines

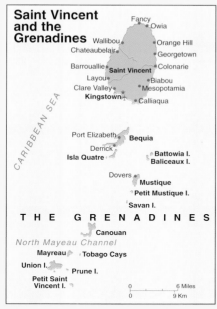

Fancy
Owia
Wallibou
Orange Hill
Chateaubelair
Georgetown
Barrouallie
Saint Vincent
Colonarie
Layou
Biabou
Clare Valley
Mesopotamia
Kingstown
Calliaqua

CARIBBEAN SEA

Port Elizabeth
Bequia
Derrick
Isla Quatre
Battowia I.
Baliceaux I.
Dovers
Mustique
Petit Mustique I.
Savan I.

THE GRENADINES

Canouan
North Mayeau Channel
Mayreau
Tobago Cays
Union I.
Prune I.
Petit Saint Vincent I.

0   6 Miles
0   9 Km

Saint Vincent and the Grenadines

Status:	Constitutional Monarchy
Area:	151 square miles
Population:	100,000
Capital:	Kingstown
Languages:	English, French patois
Currency:	Eastern Caribbean dollar (100 cents)

Saint Vincent and the Grenadines

This small country consists of the island of Saint Vincent and the northern-most islands of the Grenadines group, including Union and Bequia. Bananas and arrowroot are the primary export crops. Tourism is essential to the economy, and some of the smaller islands are the lavish hideaways of the world's wealthy.

Grenada

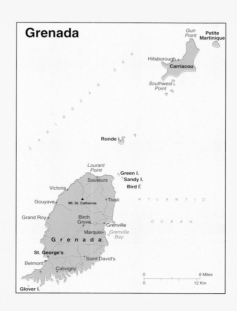

Gun Point
Petite Martinique
Hillsborough
Carriacou
Southwest Point

Ronde i.

Laurant Point
Green I.
Sauteurs
Sandy I.
Bird I.
Victoria
Gouyave
Mt. St. Catherine
Tivoli
Grand Roy
ATLANTIC OCEAN
Birch Grove
Grenville
Marquis
Grenville Bay
Grenada
St. George's
Saint David's
Belmont
Calivigny
Glover I.

0   8 Miles
0   12 Km

Grenada

Status:	Constitutional Monarchy
Area:	131 square miles
Population:	100,000
Capital:	Saint George's
Languages:	English, French patois
Currency:	Eastern Caribbean dollar (100 cents)

Grenada

An independent nation since 1974, this island country includes the island of Grenada and the southern islands of the Grenadines, the largest of which is Carriacou. Grenada is the world's foremost producer of nutmeg and mace. Other exports include bananas, citrus fruits, and cacao beans.

Barbados

0   3 Miles
0   4 Km
Greenidge
Spring Hall
Nesfield
ATLANTIC
Mile and a Quarter
Portland
OCEAN
Speightstown
Greenland
Belleplaine
Bruce Vale
Bathsheba
Westmorland
Hillcrest
Chimborazo
Saint Elizabeths
Holetown
Sturges
Blackmans
Coach Hill
Bennetts
Prospect
Reeds Hill
Belair
Massiah
Thicket
Hothersal Turning
Warrens
Turnpike
Workhall
Boarded Hall
Carrington
Six Cross Road
Carlisle Bay
Bridgetown
Saint Patricks
The Crane
Sargeant
Saint Lawrence
Providence
Charnocks
Oistins
Oistins Bay

Barbados

Status:	Constitutional Monarchy
Area:	166 square miles
Population:	300,000
Capital:	Bridgetown
Language:	English
Currency:	Barbados dollar (100 cents)

Barbados

Barbados has a warm, pleasant climate that supports a growing tourist industry. Nearly 500,000 visitors a year come mainly from the United States and Britain. Sugar and sugar products such as molasses and rum are important agricultural exports, but the island is also developing new industries such as banking and data processing. Barbados is one of the most densely populated countries in the world but has good health and educational systems.

The Netherlands Antilles, Aruba, Trinidad and Tobago

The Netherlands Antilles consists of two groups of islands 500 miles apart. The two largest islands, Curaçao and Bonaire, lie about 50 miles off the coast of the South American nation of Venezuela. The other territory lies at the northern end of the Leeward Islands, about 160 miles east of Puerto Rico. Comprised of the southern part of Saint Martin Island and the islands of Saba and Saint Eustatius, the Netherlands Antilles is a self-governing entity of the Kingdom of the Netherlands.

Trinidad and its tiny companion Tobago lie a few miles off the coast of Venezuela. The islands have high mountains in the north and lower ranges of hills across the central and southern regions. Between these highlands sit broad plains and swamps. Nearly half the island nation is forest. Islanders grow sugarcane, coffee, cacao beans, rubber, and tropical fruits for export, but the islands' main wealth comes from oil and natural gas and from the petrochemical industries based on those resources. Trinidad is also the world's largest source of asphalt—a thick, tarry substance used internationally for paving roads. Food processing, cement making, and textiles are other major employers.

Aruba sits 48 miles west of Curaçao and until 1986 was also part of the Netherlands Antilles. The island was scheduled to achieve full independence in 1996, but the people chose instead to remain a self-governing part of the Kingdom of the Netherlands. Many Arubans and citizens of the Netherlands Antilles work in tourism, banking, and other financial services, all of which are essential island industries. The islands have no mineral resources and no industries apart from local crafts. Local businessowners operate refineries that process Venezuelan oil for export, mainly to the Netherlands. Other mineral exports include phosphates from Curaçao and salt from Bonaire. The islands are not very fertile, growing only sorghum, groundnuts, aloes, and tropical fruits.

Netherlands

Status:	Self-governing Region of the Kingdom of the Netherlands
Area:	309 square miles
Population:	200,000
Capital:	Willemstad
Languages:	Dutch, English, Spanish, and Papiamento
Currency:	Guilder (100 cents)

Netherlands Antilles

Nearly 80 percent of the population lives on the largest island, Curaçao. The standard of living is high, with efficient health services and schools and almost 100-percent literacy. The soils are too poor for large-scale farming, but tourism, banking, and industries ensure a high rate of employment.

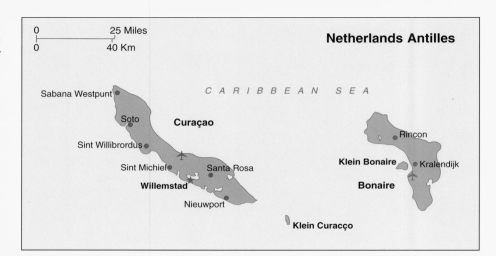

Netherlands Antilles

0   25 Miles
0   40 Km

CARIBBEAN SEA

Sabana Westpunt
Soto
Curaçao
Sint Willibrordus
Sint Michiel
Santa Rosa
Willemstad
Nieuwport
Klein Curacço

Rincon
Klein Bonaire • Kralendijk
Bonaire

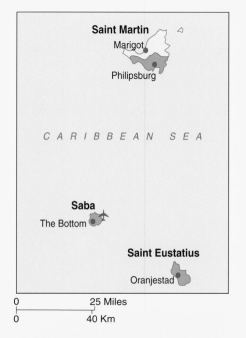

Saint Martin
Marigot
Philipsburg

CARIBBEAN SEA

Saba
The Bottom

Saint Eustatius
Oranjestad

0   25 Miles
0   40 Km

Aruba

Status:	Self-governing Island of the Kingdom of the Netherlands
Area:	75 sq mi
Population:	69,000
Capital:	Oranjestad
Languages:	Dutch, English, Spanish, and Papiamento
Currency:	Aruban florin (100 cents)

Aruba

Aruba

Almost half the people of Aruba are descended from the Arawak Indians, the island's original inhabitants. On most Caribbean islands, the Indians were wiped out by European settlers or by the diseases they brought to the islands. The modern Aruban economy depends on oil refining, fertilizer production, food exports, and tourism.

Trinidad and Tobago

Status:	Republic
Area:	1,981 square miles
Population:	1.3 million
Capital:	Port-of-Spain
Languages:	English, French, Spanish, Hindi
Currency:	Trinidad and Tobago dollar (100 cents)

Trinidad

Tobago

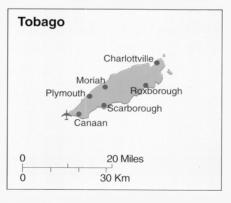

Below: Trinidad is one of the world's main producers of asphalt—a sticky black tarlike material used for surfacing roads. The asphalt occurs naturally—oozing up through the ground. Eighty percent of the island's international trade comes from asphalt.

Trinidad and Tobago

Trinidad's population is 43 percent Afro-Caribbean, 40 percent East Indian, and 16 percent mixed background. Settlers from Europe, China, the Middle East, and elsewhere comprise the other 1 percent. This blend reflects the island's colonial past, when huge plantations produced sugarcane for Spanish, French, and British owners. The economy combines agriculture, tourism, financial services, and petrochemical industries.

Glossary

abyssal plain: a vast, fairly level, and very deep area of the ocean floor where no light penetrates

archipelago: a group of islands that stretches across a sea

coniferous: describing mainly evergreen trees that bear cones and have needle-shaped leaves

continental shelf: the seabed that borders the continents and that is covered by shallow water

coral reef: a ridge of rocklike formations made up of billions of coral polyp skeletons

deciduous: describing trees that lose their leaves at some season of the year

fjord: a long, narrow sea inlet bordered by steep cliffs

fossil fuels: substances, such as coal and petroleum, that slowly developed from the remains of living things

geothermal energy: energy produced by the heat of the earth's interior

mestizo: a person of Spanish and native Indian ancestry

muskeg: a bog in northern North America

separatist: an advocate of independence or self-rule for one's group. Separatists want representatives of their own group to make the political decisions that affect the group and work to withdraw from any other political entity to which they are joined.

tundra: a region of treeless plains and permanently frozen soil around the Arctic Circle

Right: Bryce Canyon National Park, Utah

Index

A

Alaska, 12, 16, 19
Anguilla, 39
Antigua and Barbuda, 38
Appalachian Mountains, 6
Arctic Mid-Ocean Ridge, 8
Arctic Ocean, 6, 8, 12
Arctic plants and animals, 6, 8, 10
Arctic regions, 8-9; industries of, 8, 10
Aruba, 44-45

B

Bahamas, 26-27
Barbados, 40-41, 43
Bermuda, 26-27

C

Canada, 6, 8, 10, 12-15; industries of, 14; land use in, 12, 14; settlement of, 14; weather patterns of, 12
Canadian Archipelago, 8-9
Caribbean, 26-45; industries of, 26, 28, 30-31, 32, 34-35, 36, 44-45; settlement of, 26, 30, 32, 36, 40, 44-45; weather patterns of, 26, 28, 30, 32, 34, 36
Cayman Islands, 30-31
coral reefs, 26
Cuba, 26, 28-29

D

Denmark, 10
Dominica, 42
Dominican Republic, 32-33

F

Faeroe Islands, 10-11

G

geothermal energy, 10
Great Plains, 6, 18
Greenland, 8, 10-11
Grenada, 43
Guadeloupe, 39

H

Haiti, 32-33

I

ice cap, 10-11
Iceland, 10-11

J

Jamaica, 30-31

L

land area, total, 6
Leeward Islands, 36-37

M

Martinique, 42
Mexican Highlands, 6
Mexico, 6, 22-25; brief history of, 24; industries of, 24; population density of, 25; weather patterns of, 22, 23
Mexico, Gulf of, 6, 16
Mid-Atlantic Ridge, 10
Montserrat, 39

N

Netherlands Antilles, 44
New England, 6, 18
North America, 6, 10-25; land use in, 10, 12, 14, 20; settlement of, 14, 18, 21; weather patterns of, 12, 18, 20, 22, 23
North Pole, 8

P

Pacific Ocean, 12
population, total, 6
Puerto Rico, 34-35

R

Rocky Mountains, 6, 12, 18
Russia, 8, 12, 16

S

Saint Kitts and Nevis, 39
Saint Lucia, 42
Saint Vincent and the Grenadines, 43
Sierra Madre, 22

T

tourism, 6, 19, 26, 27, 30-31, 32, 36, 38-39, 42, 43, 44, 45
Trinidad and Tobago, 44-45
tundra, 6, 8, 12
Turks and Caicos Islands, 26-27

U

United States, 6, 12, 16-21; brief history of, 21; industries of, 16, 18-19; land use in, 20; rainfall in, 20; settlement of, 18, 21; territorial expansion of, 21; weather patterns of, 18, 20

V

Virgin Islands, British, 38
Virgin Islands, U.S., 38
volcanic activity, 10, 40

W

Windward Islands, 40-41